SOMALI IMMIGRANTS
IN THEIR SHOES

BY PATRICIA HUTCHISON

Published by The Child's World®
1980 Lookout Drive • Mankato, MN 56003-1705
800-599-READ • www.childsworld.com

Content Consultant: Dr. Kebba Darboe, Professor of Ethnic Studies, Minnesota State
University, Mankato

Photographs ©: Dawn Villella/AP Images, cover, 1; Sayyid Azim/AP Images, 6, 8; David
Brauchli/AP Images, 10, 12; Craig Lassig/AP Images, 14; Jonathan Alpeyrie/Polaris/
Newscom, 16, 22; Jim Mone/AP Images, 18; Red Line Editorial, 20; Eric Miller/Reuters/
Newscom, 24; Joel Koyama/MCT/Newscom, 27; Aaron Lavinsky/Star Tribune/AP
Images, 28

ISBN 9781503820319
LCCN 2016960931

Printed in the United States of America
PA02338

ABOUT THE AUTHOR

Patricia Hutchison is a former classroom teacher. She has written several
nonfiction children's books about science, nature, and history. She lives in
South Carolina with her husband. They love to travel throughout the United
States and to other countries.

TABLE OF CONTENTS

FAST FACTS

Important Numbers

- In 1990, the total number of Somali immigrants to the United States was approximately 2,500.

- By 2015, the number had grown to nearly 150,000.

Why Somali Immigrants Left

- A violent civil war and widespread famine caused many Somalis to leave their country beginning in 1991.

- Somali children under the age of 18 are the largest group among **refugees**.

Where Somali Immigrants Settled

- Today, Minnesota is home to the largest Somali population in the United States. Many Somali immigrants live in Minneapolis and Saint Paul, which are known as the Twin Cities.

- Somali immigrants have opened hundreds of small businesses in the Twin Cities.

- Other Somali immigrants have settled in Columbus, Ohio; Seattle, Washington; Atlanta, Georgia; and Washington, DC.

TIMELINE

1988: Somali president Siad Barre orders his armies to poison the well water of groups that oppose him.

1991: The government of Somalia falls apart. Barre leaves the country with his army.

1992: Approximately 300,000 Somalis die of starvation by the end of the year.

1992: Somali refugees begin to arrive in the United States.

1999: Approximately 29,000 Somali immigrants are living in Minnesota.

2001: War and starvation have created nearly 300,000 Somali refugees worldwide.

2006: War erupts again in Somalia. In Mogadishu, the country's capital, two-thirds of the people abandon the city.

2010: Approximately 60,000 Somali immigrants are living in Minnesota.

2015: Approximately 150,000 Somali immigrants are living in the United States.

Chapter 1

LIVING IN WAR-TORN SOMALIA

Bullets whizzed past the children's heads as they grasped their parents' hands. The family ran through the streets, desperately searching for safety. They were not sure if they would survive. Beginning in 1991, this was a common scene in Somalia. A civil war was causing chaos in the small East African country. People cried in horror as **rebel** soldiers destroyed their homes.

Life in Somalia wasn't always torn apart by war. The parents and their two children once lived in a sturdy house. They worked in the garden, growing flowers and vegetables. The children studied in school and played soccer. Their evenings included games of cards and dominoes. After sunset, they prayed together at the mosque.

Fridays were a day of rest. Sometimes the whole family dressed up and traveled to the capital city of Mogadishu. They ate at cafés that lined the paved roads. The parents enjoyed movies, plays, and concerts. Twice a year, the children attended a school field trip to the beach. The family, like most Somalis, felt their lives were comfortable.

Everything changed in 1991. Somalia's central government fell apart, and the president was forced out of office. Somalia is a nation of clans, which are groups of related families. These family ties date back hundreds of years. The government appointed a new president, but a leader from a different clan also claimed power. These groups battled for control of the country. Suddenly people hated their own neighbors. Different clans formed rebel groups and started fighting with each other. Rebuilding the government seemed impossible.

▲ **Rebels celebrate after taking over
Somalia's main airport.**

The children, along with their classmates, started to realize that they belonged to different clans. Even though they spoke the same language and went to the same schools, they were somehow different now. The children read the **propaganda** that was spread to make sure they knew the differences between clans. They saw fights break out between children who had once been best friends. The son later said, "This was the saddest thing I had experienced so far."[1] The parents became suspicious of their neighbors. Who was working with the rebels? Who was fighting for the government? People no longer trusted each other.

Store owners refused to sell goods to people from different clans. The family could not get the food and supplies they needed. The children were hungry. Then things got even worse. The family watched in fear as soldiers armed with guns and knives attacked their neighborhood. The rebels stole livestock and blocked food shipments.

Bombs went off nearby, and the family's home was destroyed. Feeling happy to be alive, they were forced to move in with neighbors. But soon they were living in dreadful surroundings. "Many people were living in crowded conditions," the father said. "The **hygiene** was so bad that I could see sewage running in front of my house."[2] Realizing peace would not come soon, the family wondered whether they should leave Somalia.

"When the bombs went off, people fled for their lives. I was caught in the crossfire and fled to the countryside, leaving behind my family and home. I left with nothing but the clothes on my back, lacking money, food, or **provisions** of any kind."

—Ismail M. Gorse, a Somali refugee[3]

Chapter 2

FLEEING SOMALIA

Should they stay, or should they go? The family was torn by their options. Like some of their neighbors, they held out hope for the end of the war. They prayed every day for peace. If they decided to leave, they would have to face many challenges. For example, would they have enough money to pay for transportation and food? Even if they did, where would they go? And would they make it there safely?

Bombs, bullets, death, and destruction became a daily fact of life for the family. They saw their neighbors tearfully loading into trucks and fleeing the only homes they had ever known. Some of the men stayed back to protect the family property. The family decided that if they were leaving, they would all go together.

The family stashed what they could into suitcases and bags. They took only what was necessary for survival. A truck sat at the entrance to their village. The parents and their two children climbed on. They didn't even ask where the truck was going. They were just thankful to be alive.

The journey was painfully slow. They had to take rugged roads through the wilderness instead of using the main highways. The family prayed they would not be attacked by soldiers or robbers along the way. At one point, the truck joined a group of 18 others. They stopped at night to rest. Each new day, they rambled on, hearing gunshots fired closer and closer.

At last, the truck crossed into the neighboring country of Kenya. The family looked out over acres of desert dotted with white tents. They joined the long line of refugees waiting for security clearance. Armed Administration Police searched them to make sure they were not carrying any weapons.

▲ **A mother cares for her child at a refugee camp in Kenya.**

Each family member was given a piece of paper with a number on it. Their names didn't seem to matter anymore. When they needed food, they gave their numbers to the authorities dishing it out. The family set up the two tents they were given and started their new lives as refugees. Each day, it was "normal for one to spend half the day under the scorching sun waiting for the **rations** of corn, beans, rice, and cooking fat."[4] Then the son stood in a different line to get water for the family. The family felt disgusted by the lack of proper hygiene. They prayed they would not get any of the diseases raging through the camps.

The family didn't feel much safer in the camp than they had felt back home. Violent gangs swept through and robbed people.

Neighboring citizens attacked the camp, slashing refugees with large knives. They shouted, "Get out of my country, you blood-thirsty people!"[5] Still fearing for their lives, the family decided to leave Africa.

In 1992, the United States had begun welcoming Somali refugees. Hoping to be chosen, the family went through long interviews with U.S. government officials. They had to answer many questions. Why did they choose to apply to go to the United States? What did they think would happen if the family returned to Somalia? Did they know anyone who belonged to a terrorist group? At last, after several months, they received the letter they had been hoping for. The family was approved to resettle in the United States. The letter did not say how long they would have to wait. Still, they were thankful.

A year after arriving at the camp, the mother gave birth to another daughter. Every day, the father hoped he would see their names on the list of flights to the United States. They watched as more camp neighbors were allowed to leave. After two long years of waiting, he finally saw the good news. They were on the flight list.

A few months later, the five family members boarded their plane. Butterflies fluttered in their stomachs as they rose above the clouds. Their feelings were a mixture of excitement and fear.

Chapter 3

COMING TO AMERICA

The family was exhausted when they finally landed at Minneapolis–Saint Paul International Airport. They had been traveling for more than 24 hours. It was past 11 o'clock on a cold February night in Minnesota. But as the five family members stepped off the plane, they were thrilled to see so many people there to greet them. They recognized the faces of some of their neighbors from the refugee camp in Kenya.

◀ The climate in Minnesota is much colder than the climate in Somalia.

Relatives also met them, giving hugs to the older son and his two younger sisters. "Welcome to America!" said one of their cousins. "This is a nice place. There's good education for the kids. You'll get a good job. You'll have a good life."[6]

The father said hello, in Somali, to the family's **caseworker** from the Minnesota Council of Churches. This resettlement agency was one of the few that had an agreement with the U.S. government to help Somali families immigrating to the United States. The caseworker drove them to their new home in the suburbs of Minneapolis. As part of her job, she had rented the small house for the family. She promised to return the next day.

The three children woke up early the next morning. With their faces pressed against the window, they stared at the white ground. It was the first time they had seen snow. Begging to go out and play in it, they sighed when their father said it was too dangerous.

Soon they noticed a car pulling up to the house. Their caseworker had returned. She drove the family to Minneapolis so they could apply for Social Security cards. They needed these cards to register the children in school. They would also use the cards to apply for assistance with food and health care.

▲ **Somali American children play in their home in Minneapolis.**

The five family members entered the government building. They sat in the waiting room until their number was called. This scene brought back memories of waiting in long lines at the refugee camp in Kenya.

A few days later, the parents rode the bus to the caseworker's office. The caseworker explained how much money the family would receive for food and rent. This help from the government would last for 90 days. The father prayed he would have a good job before then. Keeping with Somali tradition, he did not want his wife to get a job. He wanted her to take care of the children and their new home. The caseworker said the father would receive help from a job counselor, and both parents would attend English classes. Their children would also begin school.

The father started his **orientation** class the next day. For three weeks, he practiced interacting with others in the community, including store owners and police officers. He practiced riding the bus around town. He learned how to write checks. With the help of his job coach, he practiced job interviews. The father learned about the importance Americans place on shaking hands and smiling.

Language was the family's biggest barrier. "Everything you need you have to ask for," the father recalled later. "You are like a little kid that cannot even speak. . . . I couldn't even ask where to go. . . . I just knew to say, 'Hi.'"[7] So, the family studied English often. They wanted to learn the language as quickly as possible.

One morning, the family dressed in their best clothes. Their caseworker picked them up and took them to the school.

The son and older daughter had not studied for several years. The younger daughter, who was born in the refugee camp, had never been to school. The principal greeted the family when they arrived, and she invited them into her office for a meeting. The children would be placed in the grade levels appropriate for their ages, she said. The children were nervous, knowing they would be well behind the other students.

On a Monday in March, the three siblings held hands as they walked uneasily to school on their first day. They met other students lugging heavy backpacks. But they felt out of place because they carried nothing.

Things did not get any easier when they got to school. The son later said, "I remember when I went to school the first day . . . literally, you are deaf. That's how I felt because you'd be seeing teachers talking. . . . Can you imagine just sitting there without knowing what they are talking about?"[8]

The older daughter had a difficult day, too. At roll call, the teacher had trouble pronouncing her name. The other students laughed. They stared at her hijab, a traditional scarf that covered her head. She was not used to sitting all day long. And she was stunned by the amount of work she had to do in so many different subjects. Already, she started to feel like a failure.

◄ **Younger immigrants often have an easier time adjusting to life in the United States than their older siblings do.**

SOMALI IMMIGRANTS IN THE UNITED STATES

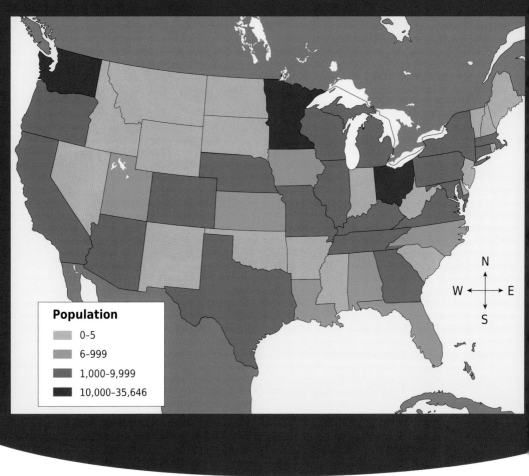

Population
- 0–5
- 6–999
- 1,000–9,999
- 10,000–35,646

The first day was a bit easier for the younger daughter. When she arrived home, she told her family, "I seen a lot of kids skipping, so I just started skipping with them."[9]

The family's caseworker helped the children adjust to their new school. She hosted a workshop for the family and other immigrants. They learned about school culture and how important it was for parents to be involved.

The caseworker also held a workshop for the teachers and administrators at the school. When it was over, the teachers had a better understanding of Somali culture. They also learned about the environment the new students had grown up in.

After a few weeks, the caseworker placed the children in the Nabad program. This was a program started by the school district to help the wave of Somali children entering the Minneapolis schools. The children would have interpreters to help them until they learned English. They would also have a chance to learn more about living in the United States. The older children were especially relieved.

However, the father felt their 90 days of help ticking away. Would they be ready when the government assistance ran out?

Chapter 4

LOOKING TO THE FUTURE

On the first day of Nabad class, the teacher called the students "super scholars." The boy grinned at the superhero mascot on his desk. The older girl's ears perked up every time she heard someone speaking Somali. Their interpreters helped the children understand what was written in their *In the USA* textbooks.

Four weeks had gone by. The father often thought about what life had been like at the refugee camp. Every day was the same. They ate rations. They waited in line for water. If they were sick, they went to the only health clinic available. But in the United States, they had to make so many decisions each day. Where should he apply for a job? Which bus should he take to the city? Should they buy cornflakes or oatmeal? Even small choices made him weary.

Toward the end of March, the children burst through the front door, eager to share what they had learned that day. They froze when they saw the frowns on their parents' faces. They were sitting at the kitchen table with their caseworker. The father asked why there had been fewer appointments lately. The caseworker explained that more refugees had arrived. She was busy helping them get started. "When you're first here, we see you a lot. But a lot of times at this point we have to say, 'I'm sorry, I can't help.'"[10]

The father was upset. "If we are left and we are not working, we can't even pay the rent," he said. "I will lose my reputation in the U.S."[11] In the camp, he had heard that if he got behind, the landlord would toss them and their belongings into the street. He pictured them all sitting on the curb.

He told the caseworker that their assistance dollars had not gone far that month. They had no money left to buy vegetables and meat. All they had left to eat was pasta and rice. The caseworker asked him whether they had bought other things besides food that month. The father confessed that he had been longing for the sense of community he had felt in Somalia. He had gone to the Somali mall in town and bought a rug. The agency would chip in more money for the April rent, she said. They could use some of the rent money to buy food. The caseworker encouraged them to reach out to their family and friends for help.

"As the 'salad bowl' theory of American integration suggests, America is a multicultural society. The various communities come together with their distinct cultures, traditions and lifestyles—much like salad ingredients—and this is what gives the U.S. its freshness and flavor."

—Somali American author Hamse Warfa[12]

The next morning, the father dressed in his only business suit. His relatives told him he should not wear his dress-like **macawis**.

◀ **Children play basketball at a park near their home.**

He took the bus to another job interview. This was the fourth one in the past two weeks.

A few days later, the father received good news. He had been hired at a meat processing plant. His first day on the new job, he grabbed at the collar around his neck. The new uniform made his skin feel itchy. But relief showed on his face as he said goodbye to his family. Although the pay wasn't great, he felt things were finally turning around for the family.

In April, the mother began a part-time job working at a daycare center. She longed for Africa and the days she spent cooking and talking with the other mothers. But she was happy she would earn money to help her family.

In late May, their caseworker knocked on their door one last time. The mother ushered her in and began to do some of the talking. She was worried about high utility bills. The caseworker assured her that the bills would soon drop since the weather was getting warmer. Then the caseworker handed the father a stack of papers. His eyebrows creased with worry. He knew that signing these papers would close their case with the agency. Then he signed the papers, knowing he had little choice. The family waved goodbye to the caseworker as she left.

Some radio programs in the Twin Cities have ▶ Somali American hosts.

In August, the father thought about the family's situation. His worst fears had not come true. They still had a solid roof over their heads. He and his wife were making enough money to pay the bills and buy food. When the children came home from school, everyone quizzed each other on the new English words they had learned. They were making good progress.

Soon it was the family's turn to welcome a cousin from Somalia. At the airport, the father hugged the cousin tightly. "We have been so lucky," the father said.[13]

THINK ABOUT IT

- What would it be like to leave the only home you have ever known and move to a foreign country?
- What would you do if you saw a girl being picked on in school for wearing a hijab?
- Some Americans do not want the U.S. government to allow Somali immigrants to come here. Do you agree with them? Why or why not?

◄ **After winning an election in 2016, Ilhan Omar became the first Somali American lawmaker in the United States.**

GLOSSARY

caseworker (KAYS-wur-ker): A caseworker is a person whose job is to help people adjust to new situations. The caseworker helped the immigrants learn how to get around the city.

hygiene (HY-jeen): Hygiene is the practice of basic cleanliness. Hygiene was so poor in the refugee camps that many people got diseases.

macawis (ma-HUH-wis): A macawis is clothing that wraps around the waist and the upper part of the body. The father's relatives told him not to wear his macawis to the job interview.

orientation (or-ee-en-TAY-shun): Orientation is a series of meetings that provide training in something new. The father attended orientation meetings to learn how to adjust to life in the United States.

propaganda (prah-puh-GAN-duh): Propaganda is information that is spread by an organization to make people believe in a certain cause. Propaganda about other clans made many Somalis lose trust in each other.

provisions (pro-VI-zhunz): Provisions are necessary items such as food and clothing. Rebels blocked shipments of provisions, so many Somalis went hungry.

rations (RA-shunz): Rations are limited amounts of food given out in a time of emergency. Refugees were given numbers that they used to claim rations in the camps.

rebel (REB-ul): A rebel is someone who fights against his or her government. The rebel soldier fought against the president's army.

refugees (ref-yoo-JEEZ): Refugees are people who seek safety in a foreign country, especially to avoid war or other dangers. The refugees were given small tents to live in.

SOURCE NOTES

1. Hamse Warfa. *America Here I Come: A Somali Refugee's Quest for Hope.* Minneapolis, MN: Sunshine Publishing, 2014. Print. 28.

2. Ismail M. Gorse. "The Life Experiences of Ethiopian Somali Refugees: From Refugee Camp to America." *UST Research Online.* University of St. Thomas, 29 Mar. 2011. Web. 15 Nov. 2016.

3. Ibid.

4. Hamse Warfa. *America Here I Come: A Somali Refugee's Quest for Hope.* Minneapolis, MN: Sunshine Publishing, 2014. Print. 66.

5. Ibid. 73.

6. Mila Koumpilova. "Years with No Nation, 90 Days to Become a Minnesotan." *StarTribune.* StarTribune, 28 Aug. 2016. Web. 15 Nov. 2016.

7. "You Are Like a Little Kid That Cannot Even Speak." *Minnesota Historical Society.* Minnesota Historical Society, n.d. Web. 15 Nov. 2016.

8. Ibid.

9. "Young People Are Not Losing Culture, but They Are Entwining with American Culture." *Minnesota Historical Society.* Minnesota Historical Society, n.d. Web. 15 Nov. 2016.

10. Mila Koumpilova. "Years with No Nation, 90 Days to Become a Minnesotan." *StarTribune.* StarTribune, 28 Aug. 2016. Web. 15 Nov. 2016.

11. Ibid.

12. Hamse Warfa. *America Here I Come: A Somali Refugee's Quest for Hope.* Minneapolis, MN: Sunshine Publishing, 2014. Print. 134.

13. Allie Shah. "Minnesota Painter's Art Captures Scenes of Prewar Somalia." *StarTribune.* Star Tribune, 1 June 2015. Web. 15 Nov. 2016.

TO LEARN MORE

Books

K'Naan. *When I Get Older: The Story behind "Wavin' Flag."* Toronto, ON: Tundra, 2012.

Mohamed, Farah M. *Somali Children's Stories: Collection of Somali Stories.* Alexandria, VA: Somali Media, 2014.

St. John, Warren. *Outcasts United: The Story of a Refugee Soccer Team That Changed a Town.* New York, NY: Delacorte, 2012.

Web Sites

Visit our Web site for links about Somali immigrants:

childsworld.com/links

Note to Parents, Teachers, and Librarians: We routinely verify our Web links to make sure they are safe and active sites. So encourage your readers to check them out!

INDEX